WORLD SERIOUS

One San Francisco Giants
Fan's 2012 Pilgrimage

Paul Kocak

Kocak Wordsmiths Ink

Copyright © 2012 by Paul Kocak

ISBN-13: 978-0615742885
ISBN-10: 0615742882

Cover photo:
Katie or Sarah or Danielle in the bleachers

Imprint logo:
leonard assante :: assante design inc.

Digital design and layout:
Becky's Graphic Design

Kocak Wordsmiths Ink
347 Whittier Avenue
Syracuse, NY 13204

To Craig, and all at The Flap

Prologue

BY THE RIVERS OF BABYLON

Why would someone jump on a jet plane just to be in the same city as his favorite baseball team more than 3,000 miles away? It's a fair question. A partial answer is supplied by a geography of the heart. Perform a Google Maps search of my soul and you will see aerial views of Stamford, Connecticut; an area of Manhattan, New York, known as Coogan's Bluff; Syracuse, New York; and San Francisco, California. Zoom in and you will see backyards, schoolyards, and ballparks. Drill down even closer with a dose of imagination and you will see a father pitching to his sons, and brothers "having a catch," to use the local phrase. But we are not conjuring up a time machine. This is not science fiction, or even baseball fiction.

So why *did* I fly at a moment's notice in October 2012 from Syracuse to San Francisco? My beloved San Francisco Giants were in the World Series. Isn't that reason enough? Wouldn't any fan do the same if he or she got the chance, no matter the cost in time or money?

Let's clear a few things up. I do not claim to be the most ardent, most faithful, most informed, most steady, or longest-running fan of Major League Baseball's San Francisco Giants. Nothing like that. Most of you reading this can lay claim to watching more Giants games in person or on TV or online. I have no problem with that. I shake your hand — and salute you, just like Angel Pagan's trademark gesture. This is not a contest for fan supremacy. If it were, I would surrender. You would win.

This is a World Series saga from the perspective of one fan. It is neither a play-by-play account nor a statistical analysis. The only sabermetrics come from the algorithm of my heart and soul. If you nod your head, even slightly, and say to yourself, "Yeah, I get it. I could see myself doing that," then I have succeeded. At best, we are compatriots. We are jubilant fellow citizens of Giants Nation, wearers of the Black and Orange. And when our team wins the World Series, we are Bask Separatists, soaking in the sunny rays of victory during a long winter, right through to the end of the next season, when we either repeat as World Champions or another team wrests the crown from us. At the least, we are fellow baseball fans, fellow readers of personal history, or curious observers of human obsession and devotion.

As I was finishing this book, I saw NBA legend Dolph Schayes walk into Le Moyne Plaza, a comfortable workspace with free wi-fi and featuring the Le Moyne College (my alma mater) bookstore, a donut shop, and a pizza place. I walked up to Mr. Schayes as he pored over the New York Times. With little introduction, I engaged him in conversation about ballet. In the summer of 2011 my daughter Evelyn Kocak, a dancer with Pennsylvania Ballet, had taught his granddaughter Hannah at Syracuse University's Summer Dance Intensive. This enabled me to converse easily with the basketball Hall of Famer who continues to make his home in Syracuse after his professional career. In no time at all, I found Dolph Schayes to be urbane, elegant, cordial, and unassuming. I soon turned the conversation to baseball. (Of course.) I did not ask for his autograph — in my later years I tend to place less value in such things — but gave him a copy of my book *Baseball's Starry Night*, and inscribed it with some words about "talking baseball." But here's the thing: Schayes told me he grew up in the Bronx, by 183rd Street, not quite two miles from Yankee Stadium. But he was not a Yankees fan. He was a fan of the St. Louis Browns. "I might have been the only St. Louis Browns fan in all of New York City," he mused. Why a team so far away? Schayes said he liked the Browns because of their brown and orange uniforms. Their uniforms were more colorful than the drab and muted flannels of the day. And he liked the players. They were underdogs. Schayes readily recited the starting lineup of the 1944 Browns, top to bottom. He told me about pitchers Sig Jakucki (noting his 13-9 record) and Jack Kramer, and one-armed outfielder Pete Gray. He rightly remembered (naturally, afterward I scoured the Internet to confirm his recollection) that Jakucki beat the Yankees to end the season to clinch the pennant for St. Louis and the novelty of the all-St. Louis series, versus the Cardinals, who won it 4 games to 2. He was right on the mark. So, I had to ask, "When the St. Louis Browns became the Baltimore Orioles, did you stick with them?" Sure enough, Dolph Schayes talked with a twinkle in his eyes about the Orioles' 2012 team and their surprisingly successful season. He mentioned injuries to Nick Markakis and Brian Roberts. Pretty alert for a fellow born in 1928.

Aside from the fact that both the Giants and Orioles share black and orange as team colors, what's the point, you ask? The answer is both simple and complex. I reflected that Schayes and I both know what it is like to live in baseball Babylon. We both understand the challenges — even the added excitement — of following a team from afar, despite impracticality or foolishness. We can't help ourselves. Yes, it would be easier to cave in to convenience. I could have surrendered and become a Mets fan. I considered it in the 1980s when I lived in New Jersey. But whenever I journeyed to Shea Stadium to see the visiting San Francisco Giants, I could not cross that line. I could not surrender my Giants passport. I could not pull the string on that pitch. For better or for worse, I am part of the Great Giants Diaspora. (Let's rephrase that: for better or for best. After all, as I write this, I bathe in the warm rays of World Championship afterglow.)

"If someone were to walk in here now wearing a Giants cap, I would go right up to them and ask them why," I told Schayes. I suspect deep down he shares that impulse: if he saw someone with an Orioles hat, he would feel a sense of camaraderie.

We shared a few stories about the Polo Grounds, he with more validity than I. He had seen the Giants play Sunday double-headers there and was present on V-J Day, when the end of World War II was celebrated. As for myself, I caught the Mets in 1962 losing two games to the St. Louis Cardinals, with Stan Musial homering three times. I never saw the Giants play in the Polo Grounds, though my childish imagination pictured Willie Mays roaming its outfield meadows and heard ghostly echoes of Russ Hodges's immortal pennant call in 1951.

Real life offers literal poetry if we but look for it. Symmetry abounds. My encounter with Dolph Schayes, as serendipitous as it was, sheds light on why I felt compelled to see the Giants in the 2012 World Series, even though it required a transcontinental pilgrimage. Sometime after the 1954 World Series, which I have no memory of, I asked Thomas "Richard" Hayes, my half-brother, "Who do you like?" "The Giants," he answered.

That is all it took. If the Giants were good enough for him, whom I idolized, they were good enough for me. Richard joined the Air Force, our family moved to another side of town in Stamford, Connecticut, and I took up sandlot baseball and inaugurated a baseball scrapbook. Before long, my Giants abandoned me, moving to the West Coast. But mostly because of one center fielder who wore Number 24, I stayed with my team, through lean years, long distances, and three time zones.

Therefore, having relished the sights and sounds of the city of San Francisco for Game 1 of the 2010 World Series, I was tempted to relive the magic. Yet, I was conflicted because I realized that was then and this was now. I knew that 2012 was infinitely different from 2010. But different in what way? For one thing, the two World Series were played by vastly different teams who got to the pinnacle in radically different ways. Plus, I was different. As with our whole fan base, I could no longer claim to be an innocent. The Giants had finally won a championship in 2010. Could it be sweeter a second time around? I was willing to find out.

"Please have your boarding pass ready," announced the United Airlines customer service person at the gate. I was ready. I've always been ready.

Enjoy the ride.

November 30, 2012
Syracuse, N.Y.

WORLD
SERIOUS

Chapter 1

LIKE A CIRCLE 'ROUND THE SUN

Why is baseball such a big deal to me? I was not very good at it. The highest level I ever played baseball was PRE-Little League. I had a pretty good arm and no stick. As an outfielder, I resembled Charlie Brown of the Peanuts comic strip, circling under a fly ball only to have it barely miss landing on my head. Or I would eagerly anticipate a line drive, only to freeze in fear and watch it sail by me. Since I was fast and had a strong left arm, I would chase the ball down and whip it back to the infield. If I were lucky, the runner would have halted at third base. Coaches saw opportunity in my arm and put me on the pitcher's mound. No control, and nothing on my pitches. I was only 10 or 11 years old. The opposition would gleefully taunt me and chant from the bench, "Two, four, six, eight! Who do we appreciate? The pitcher!" Ungrammatical bastards. In backyard sandlot games, I was often the last kid picked, so I sat on a large boulder, with a stick in hand, and "announced" the game. You could make the mental-health claim that baseball should have been avoided, not embraced, with a personal history like this.

Why does baseball, and the San Francisco Giants in particular, pull my heartstrings, and in the case of this trip, my purse strings? As a reader of Marcel Proust, I recognize that memories are powerful but also idiosyncratic and selective. What do I remember? I remember being in a meadow on the grounds of the Stamford Museum and Nature Center, a policeman my father knew from World War II pitching to me, my brother Jack in the field, and my father's arms circling me, "like a circle 'round the sun," as the song goes, his hands bracketing mine on a baseball bat. It was his swing as much as mine. It was our swing. I remember these as rare embraces, but after fifty years I wonder if they were simply better-remembered embraces. A photograph, taken by our father with a box camera, shows Jack in a Yankees uniform, posed as a batter, and me with a Giants uniform, squatting as a left-handed catcher. I remember insisting to my mother that I wear my New York Giants uniform to Franklin School, in the first grade, and later shrugging off the teacher's "punishment": "You will have to play by yourself, over there, at recess." Fine with me. I tossed a ball back and forth against the school wall, conjuring dramatic and heroic scenarios. What sort of punishment is that? Like Jack Kerouac and thousands of other kids, I invented a baseball game with a deck of cards and kept meticulous statistics. Bill Virdon was home-run king. I was the commissioner of a fantasy league before fantasy leagues existed. When Jack and I and neighbor Michael

Palo shagged fly balls over by Westover School, we pretended to be Major Leaguers, Mickey Mantle, Willie Mays, and Duke Snider, respectively.

They say the Giants won the Series in 1954. I'll take "their" word for it. I was alive, born in late 1948. I have no recollection, hazy or otherwise, of that World Series, or The Catch, or baseball via radio, television, or subterranean tremor. Check that. I must have felt the tremors, or else I would never have felt the urge to ask my brother Richard, "Who do you go for?" His assured reply of "the Giants" cast its spell. That was all it took. That might be hard to believe, but he towered above me, about to graduate from high school and enter the world. His kindness and warmth were good enough. You can let the shrinks decode why I went with Richard's choice instead of my dad's or my brother Jack's, Yankees fans both. To say that my choice of teams based on this brief exchange "held" is a textbook case of understatement.

From the outset, I wanted a scrapbook to honor my team and freeze-frame my memories. My mother and I walked down the aisle of Stamford's downtown Woolworth's, on Atlantic Street. It is superfluous to add "downtown." There was nowhere else to shop. Everyone came downtown. No strip malls, no malls, no suburban office parks. I do not know where the idea of a scrapbook came from; there was no popular craze with special accoutrements and equipment and cut-outs and stick-ons and scissors. I wanted a scrapbook for the Giants. If my father and Jack accompanied us on this trip, as was likely — after all, why not? — they may indeed have wandered along separate aisles of the linoleum floors or the wood-floor section over by the parakeets. My dad's mantra was something along the lines of "keep your hands off that" or "you're going to break it." The counters had glass walls about 5 inches tall separating the items for sale, which some twelve or thirteen years later I'd take down or reconfigure when I worked at Woolworth's on a summer job. My father had a pronounced fear of store-item breakage, rooted in Depression-era poverty fears and experience. The scrapbooks were in the photo album section. The pages were bound by tassels that you could tie or untie as you inserted or removed pages of the album, or scrapbook, if you will.

"I want that one." We bought a heavy cardboard-leatherish brown specimen. We purchased mucilage, either then or on the next trip, that came in a container with a rubber top. You turned the bottle upside down and pushed out the thick gooey glue. I glued in Topps baseball cards and newspaper articles and stuff from The Sporting News or Sports Illustrated or Sport. Such manner of affixing baseball cards allegedly prevented me from receiving hundreds of dollars decades later if I were to sell the cards, which was unlikely anyway.

After the 1957 season, the Giants not only left New York, not far from my home. They left the East Coast, for San Francisco. I tearfully witnessed fans on

TV chanting "Stay, team, stay" after the final game at the Polo Grounds, and put an article about it in my scrapbook.

Despite being abandoned, I clung to my team, not knowing what else to do. I wrote to the San Francisco Chamber of Commerce and they sent me a pamphlet about the city. It was as if I had to study the language and terrain of a new country. I was infatuated with Willie Mays. Out of desperation, I secretly tried to telephone Mays when my parents would leave the house. I was nine years old. I needed to talk to Willie, see how he was adjusting, see how things were going. I had read about some marriage trouble in Sport magazine and Sports Illustrated. I needed Mr. Mays to know we had not forgotten him back East, back in the William C. Ward homes in Stamford, Connecticut. I needed to know he was okay, and for him to know I had not forgotten him. I could not say it, but I wanted to show thanks. I cannot articulate it now, but I will try. I wanted to thank Willie Howard Mays Jr. for the pure joy and abandon he displayed, along with fierce pride and powerful motion and poetry of speed and daring. His cap flying off — stunt or not — as he rounded second or headed for deep center field, his hunched shoulders, his foot digging in at the plate, his infectious laugh, his dugout antics. All this gripped me and never let go of me, informing my attitudes toward race, sport, class, politics, and loyalty. But the long-distance operator never put me through.

Chapter 2
CLOSE ENCOUNTERS OF THE FAN KIND

A fish out of water looks for other fish. That's why my Giants' fan's antennae are sensitive and alert to simple matters such as black and orange worn together or SF on a cap or shirt. It is exceptional in Syracuse and in the Northeast, though not a total rarity. Everything gets totally out of whack if I attend a baseball game at, say, Citi Field, with the visiting Giants as I did in April 2012 or in 2009 when Matt Cain beaned David Wright. In those instances, the joint is aswarm with like-minded fans, so there are ample opportunities for connection. I don't quite know how to handle it. Back home in the 'Cuse if I am at the local mall or Alliance Bank Stadium or in historic Armory Square, I typically approach anyone wearing Giants' gear to begin an animated conversation. Let me modify that. In the last few years, I have either grown less socially awkward or cagier in this regard. I've gotten burned a few times as my family members roll their eyes thinking, "Uh-oh, there goes Dad again approaching a total stranger." The payback is frequently rewarding: a new fan connection, a story to go with it, an exchange of heartfelt fan moments. The flip side is a sour look, an angry halt to someone's gait, a perceived invasion of one's private Idaho of fan world. Sometimes the hat is worn for no reason whatsoever, possibly even owing to some recognized colors of turf and signification for gang members! Nevertheless, there are rewards. In the summer of 2012, in one of my walks through downtown Syracuse, I spied a San Francisco Giants license plate holder on a car in Franklin Square. That was a very rare find. So I wrote a note and placed it on the car's windshield. A few days later I received an email from local Giants fan Sam Piraino. (He later confessed the irony that it wasn't even his car but his son's car, and his son is a Yankees fan.) Sam, who is a registered pharmacist, texted and talked with me during the 2012 postseason, but we had never met until after the triumphant World Series. I walked into Asti's Ristorante, and he was sporting a Giants' jacket, and I had a 2010 World Series hoodie, orange. Before the server seated us — kaboom! — we here from the adjoining table: "Giants! All right!" Yikes, two attractive women, a man, an older lady. One is from San Francisco! I excitedly tell the folks at our adjoining table that Sam and I are meeting for the first time and it is only because we are Giants fans, I just went to the Series, I'm writing a book, blah blah blah. How do you plan this?! Better yet, Sam and I discover that our mothers-in-law live in the same freaking building in Kirkwood, some 70 miles away!

One of the best out-of-town-but-not-in-San Francisco fan experiences occurred in Cooperstown, New York in May 2011, when the 2010 World Series trophy made one its last stops on a long continental trip of celebration. Beth and Adrianna and I had arrived the night before, staying at a small lakeside motel up the road from Cooperstown proper. In fact, Adrianna had requested we make it her May 4 birthday present. On the night Willie Mays turned 80, on May 6, it was the eve of our trophy obeisance for which we would all receive baseball plenary indulgences — as a former Roman Catholic seminarian I cannot resist these ecclesiastical asides. The Hall of Fame on May 7, a Saturday, had a respectable showing of Giants fans buzzing through the building. We posed beside the shining trophy like pilgrims standing next to a saint's reliquary in the Sistine Chapel if they have any there. The parishioners of Giants Nation filled an auditorium at the Hall of Fame, and we were treated to a live, personally guided tour of AT&T Park via the Internet projected onto a big screen. We owned the place. Upstairs, near a display case of 2010 World Series memorabilia, we met Dennis Zucchino and Randy Wong. They are Giants fans who met in Cooperstown. Zucchino is a year or so my junior and had just retired from IBM and lives in Warwick, New York, south of the Catskills, where New York borders New Jersey and Pennsylvania. Wong was a highway patrol officer from California, a young man who spoke of many spur-of-the-moment Giants road trips. We exchanged contact information. And I cannot resist adding there was a very attractive young Asian woman who had season tickets at AT&T Park. In a very cool twist of fan fate and loyalty, she encountered a familiar face from AT&T Park: "her" regular usher from her section at the ballpark!

So, no matter what ballpark or mall or rural hamlet or major metropolis I happen to be visiting, I look for the black and orange representing our team. You never know what it might lead to (even book passages). In 2010, in Philadelphia of all places, on the same day the Giants would later clinch the pennant, I met some folks from San Francisco who had premier seats for the game. (I was to attend the ballet, to see my daughter perform. Yes, the crowd did check text messages.) This past summer, at Turner Field in Atlanta, I met Tike Narry and his family, from the Bay Area. They had been to something like 30 ballparks. (I'm up to 21.) Once, at a minor-league game in Binghamton (Madison Bumgarner hit a grand slam), I met this guy Skip, from San Jose, who had Pablo Sandoval's phone number in his cellphone. You never know. You have to be ready.

Chapter 3

A DRY RUN TO FINNERTY'S

On October 16, 2012, in the heat of the National League Championship Series, Dennis Zucchino, whom you will remember from a Cooperstown close encounter, emailed me: "Paulie, I'm going to Finnerty's for tomorrow's afternoon game ... to be with that Bay Area mood ...." We had both heard of Finnerty's because the 2010 World Series trophy made a stop there on its tour. And sis-boom-bah just like that I drove three-plus hours the next day from Syracuse to Dennis's beautiful house in Warwick, in the hills some 70 miles northwest of New York City. I met his wife, Regina, in their acclaimed garden. We exchanged pleasantries, and Dennis and I then headed into lower Manhattan to Finnerty's to watch Game 3 of the 2012 NLCS against the St. Louis Cardinals.

Let's get this straight. Two Giants fans on the less-sunny side of youth evict themselves from the coziness of their living-room couches to watch the Giants in a bar? Yes, this is what you are dealing with.

As for myself, I do not hang out in bars and I do not drink booze. The road trip to Finnerty's was a radical diversion, a sharp left turn from Serenity Drive and the comfort zone it offers. But Dennis's emailed invitation was enticing. One reason was a chance to meet him a second time. Oh. Wait. You were doing all this with a complete stranger?! Not exactly. After Dennis and I had met in May 2011, we kept in touch via occasional phone calls and emails. We also maintained an indirect contact at a digital playground-clubhouse-fan cave. At the Oneflapdown77.com blog, otherwise known as The Flap, we were — and are — part of a cyber-community of smart and sassy San Francisco Giants fans. (In fact, dear reader, you might as well assume that any "friend" or "fan" noted from here on in this narrative is likely to have ancestral lineage to The Flap.)

The decision to go to Finnerty's on a moment's notice while watching my daughter Adrianna's soccer game in Syracuse illustrates the psychological disorders and predilections of your ardent narrator. Life, interrupted. For baseball. Throw responsibility and caution to the autumnal winds. To her credit (from my vantage point), Beth, my wife, was ostensibly okay with this crazy scheme. Either that, or after all these years, she had thrown in the towel of reason or convention. Adrianna needs a ride to school? We'll ask her friend Cathy Starmer to take her. Settled. Going to Finnerty's.

Dennis and I had a grand time trekking to Gotham, driving through flickering sunlight and exchanging stories of family, baseball, work (past tense), and politics just before the 2012 presidential election. (We fortunately discovered that we share the same ideological slants and passions. And if you factor in that we are fans of a Left Coast team, you could arrive at your own conclusions. Got a problem with that?) We got to know each other. As we spied the Manhattan skyline in the distance like Oz as seen from Nutley, New Jersey, I left a cellphone voicemail message to my good friend Warren Young in Kennett Square, Pennsylvania. ("Hey, Warren, guess what? You know I was in Connecticut just a few days ago for my mom's birthday, but surprise, surprise, I'm back on the road, passing through Nutley, New Jersey, waving to your ancestors. Going to watch a baseball game at a bar in New York City. Can you believe it? Yes, you can. Crazy? Ciao.")

Walking from the garage where we parked, I was excited to spot from across the street the Giants logo on a flag or banner at Finnerty's. Finnerty's is at Second Avenue and 14th Street in lower Manhattan not far from New York University and Greenwich Village. It faces Second Avenue on the west side, and a large, open picture window permits passing pedestrians a peek at the zealots inside and a sampling of the roars erupting at unpredictable moments. It's a narrow, one-story venue, with a bar, some shelves and tables to hold drinks, and a back room with other tables. Eighteen televisions enable patrons plenty of viewing opportunities. Food does not seem to be a specialty since Dennis went down the street and bought four slices of pizza for a buck each and brought them into the place in a pizza box, and the bouncer never minded. It's the people. Who are the people?

At the outset, I was surprised that Dennis and I seemed to be the only legacy New York Giants holdovers. If we were not the oldest fans there, it was close to that. Nevertheless, Finnerty's offered us an immediate connection to Giants Nation, as if we were now hard-wired to the mother ship, not united via some flimsy Internet connection with a router that kept crashing. As the afternoon game progressed, more and more folks poured in, especially as offices neared closing time of 5 p.m. Most were young, in their twenties. From what I could discern, most were Bay Area transplants. I engaged in conversation with a handful and here are some snapshots of these denizens of Finnerty's.

As the game got under way under moody skies with a threat of storms in St. Louis's Busch Stadium, it was surreal to hear "let's go, Giants" chanted loudly. It was as if we were at AT&T Park but not quite, maybe in St. Louis sitting with fans of the visiting team, or in a Bay Area sports bar. All of that in bits and pieces, and none of that precisely. To exchange high-fives (even though I'm often more shy than that plus afraid of jinxing matters) enabled us to soak in a home-team vibe. And what did the passers-by on the Manhattan think of this sequestered invasion from an alien nation? They did not care. The Giants posed no threat to the Yankees. At that juncture, the Yankees only had to be concerned with the Detroit Tigers. We were relevant. (But we Giants fans all know how that worked out, don't we? Wink, wink, bask, bask.)

It was childishly comforting to raise my voice in a chorus with fellow Giants fans. In the third inning, Angel Pagan and Marco Scutaro had leadoff hits against Cards starter Kyle Lohse. The Finnerty's faithful burst forth with syncopated chants of MARCO (wait for it, like an echo) SCUTARO over and over as if we were near McCovey Cove, instead of Manhattan's (and New Jersey's) Hudson River. The joint was loud, boisterous and homey. I had to look out the door to check that this was New York. It is? You sure we did not take a Large Hadron Collider time-machine ride to retro-incarnate ourselves in Cali? Well, it worked because Scutaro doubled, showing no ill effects from his NLCS Game 1 collision with Matt Holliday.

The excitement felt good — even though I had a twinge a being a spy in the house of love, to use an unforgettable phrase from author Anaïs Nin. But I was hardly a covert operations agent, since I had dutifully and openly paid my dues all these years as a Giants fan going all the way back to 1955, when they resided several miles north of where I stood, at the Polo Grounds. I just wish I had encountered a few other refugees from those days to validate my Polo Groundsiness. Nevertheless, Dennis Zucchino and

I were citizens of the same alien nation. There we were. Giants fans in not-quite-exile, amid the cheers and multitudes of black-and-orange-wearing décor representing the Diehards Diaspora. (I must note there were other color variations. I chatted with one patron who had a cool and hip blue and white San Francisco Seals cap.)

In the third, the Giants took a 1-0 lead after Pablo Sandoval's groundout scored Pagan. Although I did not report this to anyone, I felt we needed more. This wasn't going to be enough. The Giants had had Pagan and Scutaro on second and third with nobody out, and this is what we came up with, one well earned but quiet run. After Buster Posey was intentionally walked, Hunter Pence, our preacher man, grounded into a double play. Inning over. Our prospects looked as glum as the Midwest sky and its advancing storms.

Between half-innings, I scouted the surroundings and looked for interview opportunities. I had three reasons for being at Finnerty's: promote my book *Baseball's Starry Night*, meet fellow Giants fans, and get material for a new book, centered on my life as a Giants fan. Oh. Right. A fourth reason: watch the actual game. During the commercial breaks, loud music played as orchestrated by a tall, imposing figure on the left side of the bar. I learned he was the owner and manager, so I approached him.

"Hi. I tweeted that I was coming down here from Syracuse," I shouted.

"I saw that," replied a welcoming Dieter Seelig. I promptly whipped out my blue Sharpie and applied it to a book. I gladly gave it to the grand master of the hoopla, the owner of Finnerty's. We shook hands firmly and exchanged contact information for potential future Giantscentric encounters.

One of the first regulars I encountered was Aron, a student transplant from San Francisco. "I first heard of Finnerty's from a stage manager who accidentally said Professor Thom's was the SF bar. My first time coming to 14th Street and 2nd Ave., I went into Prof Thom's to watch Timmy [Lincecum] pitch an awesome game." Aron soon learned that Finnerty's, next door, was the place to be. (Professor Thom's, it turns out, is a hangout for New England Patriots, Boston Red Sox, and Michigan fans, among others.) "My first memory there was the Brooks Conrad game [during the 2010 NLDS]. There was a big thunderstorm outside. At some point," recalled Aron in a later email, "the TV monitors went out, and Dieter put Kruk and Kuip on the radio. Coming from the Bay, having Kruk and Kuip call the game was better than watching anything, frankly." (Incidentally, earlier in the season in Pittsburgh, just before the All-Star break, I met Giants announcers Mike Krukow and Duane Kuiper as I was promoting my first book. They were terrific.)

In a subsequent digital conversation, Aron readily rattled off the names of the Finn's crew: Dieter and partner Brian Stapleton, as well as employees Annie, Ryan, Morgan, Brett, Patrick, Danielle, Carlos, and Jonathan — give or take. Plus, he recited a crew of regulars like a manager posting a lineup: Nate, Matt, Adam, Josh, Joey, Steph, Rachel, Mark, Edwin, Pacon, Duvall, Alena, Wally, Tierney, Kevin, John, Clark, Maddie, Mia, Natassa, and Chelsey — give or take.

Meanwhile, the game progressed as the doomer side of my fandom feared. Giants starter Matt Cain gave up a two-run homer to Matt Carpenter, subbing for Carlos Beltran. Cards up, 2-1. The place sure got quiet in a hurry. The threat of rain lurked in St. Louis; the threat of gloom loomed in my cerebral cortex. Despite such meteorological and metaphysical omens, I wandered amid the crowd. But I was more tentative than I had expected myself to be. The prospect of the Cardinals beating out the Giants and advancing to the World Series a second consecutive year must have added some stickiness to the soles of my shoes.

Meet John Chin, standing to my left. (Excuse my shouting. It's a bar. It gets loud. And forgive me if I ask you to repeat stuff.) He wore a shirt emblazoned with "#1 Dad." John claims he is 44 but could pass for someone in his thirties. Born in the Glen Park neighborhood, he is an avid Giants fan who by day is a sales and marketing manager for IZ-ON Media in San Francisco, one of many high-tech branding firms dotting the city.

"I heard about Finnerty's from my wife, who is another die-hard Giants fan from birth. She recalled hearing about this safe haven for Giants fans in NYC from Kruk and Kuip/Kuip." As it turned out, it was his first visit there, too, but you would never know it. If you were observing us, you might have concluded we were both regulars who had planned to meet there. In an email after our encounter, Chin related, "At Finnerty's the energy was exactly like at AT&T Park or a local pub in SF. Everyone knows all the player's names, each of their strengths/weaknesses, and their nicknames."

Thank you. It wasn't just me experiencing a psychotic fugue.

Chin's e-missive told tales from the heart of a fan of the sort I enjoyed collecting for *Baseball's Starry Night*. "I grew up going to as many games as possible at Candlestick with my Mom. My Dad worked two jobs to make ends meet for my large family – I have 5 siblings). We would take the bus there while still light out carrying our extra blankets and thermoses of hot chocolate. Then, we would stay after the game ended and the crowd subsided to have my Dad come pick us up with the car.

"My boys, Spencer, 11, and Darren, 8, couldn't tell you what a baseball looked like just two years ago. It wasn't until about August 2010 when the G-men were in the hunt that they started paying attention. Postseason 2010 was solely on TV for us, but the boys had the bug officially by then. We pulled them out of school for the parade and they stood in line with us for five hours just to get into AT&T Park for FanFest."

No wonder this guy caught my attention. He's my kind of fan.

"The saddest thing that I still reflect upon is that Mom loved the Giants a lot, but she passed away in January 2009 and couldn't see them win a World Series as the San Francisco Giants. I cried a lot at the 2010 parade wishing she could be there."

That's the kind of emotion I treasure. It's stories like this that made our journey to Finnerty's worth it.

But shortly after my conversation with John Chin, the long-expected rains came to St. Louis in the bottom of the seventh inning, just after a Shane Robinson single made it 3-1 Cards. Cain was out. And so was Finnerty's mostly emptied out. What to do? Dennis and I decided to head back. As it was, it might be past midnight when we got back to his house. I would go back to Syracuse the next day. During the 3-hour 28-minute rain delay, Dennis and I headed back into exurbia and the hinterland of our anxious hope. Toward the end of the trip back to Warwick, we caught bits and pieces of the game on the radio. (Don't you love hearing a baseball game on the radio?) We would talk to the radio and each other. "A little hit here, and we're back in it." But it seemed hollow. Our juju was impotent, to borrow a term from my friend Hart Seely in his hugely entertaining *The Juju Rules*. Dennis's wife Regina was still up as we strolled in to the living room, but not watching the game. (Dennis had already told me Regina is a Yankees fan, to which I wondered with wry amusement whether their household were like James Carville and Mary Matalin's, occupying polar opposites of loyalties.) Dennis frantically prevailed upon his spouse to find the game on the screen, and we caught the last Sandovalian out. We lost. Which dampened my spirits like so much rain pelting the tarps covering the infield.

The most remarkable thing about my night at Finnerty's was what I didn't do. I had talked amid the noise and music and loud game televisions with the handful of people described above, but I did not interview any of the young ladies in Giants gear. There were tons of them. Very pretty. This is not like me to pass on the opportunity to flirt, given the excuse of my role as a big-shot author searching for stories. What got into me? Maturity?

The other remarkable thing, which did not even register subconsciously, was that I had just performed a dry run. To where, I did not yet know.

Chapter 4

EPISTLE TO ETHAN

Hey, I am sorry I bopped you in the head in the back yard while we were tossing the ball around when you were — what? — twelve or thirteen. And I'm sorry it knocked your glasses off and left the imprint of the ball's stitching on your forehead. I ran over as fast as I could. At least the imprint wasn't permanent like some bizarre Frankenstein-like tattoo, thank God. And, no, I do not blame you for never having a catch again. As you can see here, I can now admit I was never much better as a baseball player. Plus, my arm was a little wild. So, I appreciate you never held it against me. If our little ill-fated game of catch thwarted any budding interest in baseball, think of all the hours I have allowed for you to indulge in other worthy pursuits, such as video games. Better yet, be grateful for all the anxiety I have spared you. I also gave you permission to live a so-called normal life free of box scores, line scores, standings, projections, Coolstandings, and Fangraphs, which as an animation and comic creator you would find decidedly dull. Finances. Deterring you from the hardball-diamond appetites has also let you foster dollars-and-cents common sense unencumbered by spending binges on hats, sweatshirts, books, key chains, or transcontinental flights.

We both can exult in knowing our baseball bond is no longer a physically perilous one. When I asked you to come up with something attractive and pleasing for the cover of *Baseball's Starry Night*, you launched a rocket that sailed over the outfield wall and out of the park, setting off those now-standard fireworks. The gorgeous cover art for the book gets as many rave reviews as the writing, maybe more. (Let's face it, it is challenging to get folks to read these days.)

Finally, if your son Jasper ever wants to "toss the old pill around" with Gramps, I promise we'll start with a tennis ball, maybe even a very small and lightweight Nerf ball. Just saying.

Love,
Dad

Chapter 5

OCTOBER SURPRISE, SURPRISE

Even miracles require planning. Before players were warming up before the first pitch of Game 7 of the National League Championship Series, on Monday, October 22, 2012, I booked a round trip to San Francisco with BTI Travel Consultants of Syracuse for an out-of-my-league $878.70. The day before, after church, I explained to fellow parishioner Yvonne Shaw, of BTI. "I want to go to San Francisco, but the Giants have to win tonight and again on Monday night. It's a long shot. But what should I do?" This was a travel dilemma. Nevertheless, asking for intervention in a church fellowship hall was apt, given the near-miraculous set of circumstances I was contemplating. Yvonne told me to call her office Monday morning, adding that she would put me in touch with the right person. By using a travel agent, I would be able to cancel my reservation without having to pay a huge penalty, just a $33 fee. On that Sunday morning, huge hurdles remained. I was reminded of them as I bet parishioner Tim Orcutt twenty-five cents that I'd make the trip, to the World Series. The small amount was not cheapness or risk aversion. I did not want to piss off any Fates that might be on my side. I was turbocharged with optimism because Barry Zito in the game of his Giants' life on Friday night had pitched the Black and Orange to a 5-0 Game 5 win, sending the series back to San Francisco. Elimination was thwarted, but the Redbirds held a 3-2 advantage in the seven-game NLCS. The Giants needed to beat the St. Louis Cardinals twice to make my trip a World Series jaunt, and not a frivolous and empty dash to San Francisco. (Or not a trip at all.) Another cause for optimism was the Giants' perfect record to date in the postseason when facing elimination: three wins against the Cincinnati Reds and one so far against the Cardinals. But could they win two more elimination games?

Did people think I was kidding? Sure, the cost was prohibitive, but I was more than half done with a rough manuscript for a more expansive version of this book, and I was not about to omit a thrilling chapter that was never in the outline, or in my 3-D-life imagination. So on Monday morning I awoke to better odds. The night before, the Gigantes' Ryan Vogelsong — himself a miracle story — beat St. Louis's cagey veteran Chris Carpenter 6-1 at AT&T Park. The NLCS was knotted at three games apiece. A Game 7 loomed. The Giants had never won a Game 7 showdown in their history! Monday morning I nervously conferred with BTI travel consultant Chrissy Davenport, and with my wife, and with my conscience. By early afternoon, I pulled the trigger and booked the flight, even though at that point one more miracle was needed. I soothed my conscience by reminding myself this venture would be a legitimate research effort for a book about my life as a Giants fan — as if that were the only nudge I needed. (To expiate my financial guilt as only someone brought up Catholic could, I sought to balance the financial and moral ledgers by going to my bank and emptying my change jar. My deposit yielded a disappointing $118.12, which minus a $9.44 counting fee, found its way into my checking account.) And when the Giants did win Game 7 and the National League pennant, baptized in a San Francisco deluge on that Monday night, I was in. There would be no airline ticket refund. The pilgrimage was on.

I had set plans a few days earlier to stay with my friend Ted Speros. He had cautioned me that space was a problem; he is a serious movie collector. DVDs abound. I told him if it was all right with him, it was okay with me. On his own initiative, Ted had sent me hard-to-find copies of the San Francisco Chronicle during the 2010 surge and for Matt Cain's perfect game. However, during Game 7 of the NLCS I emailed and talked with my friend Steve Melikean, who lives in Denver. Steve offered that his aunt, Mary Calica, has a four-story Victorian in the Sunset District of San Francisco and that she would likely be cool with having me stay there, with her two resident visitors (young ladies learning English from Germany and Switzerland),

and her two dogs, Leo and Jules. Sounded good. In my conversations with Steve, I importuned upon Steve to rendezvous with me at Aunt Mary's, since we had only emailed, Skyped, and called each other previous to this. In short order, the living arrangements at Aunt Mary's were set. I got to chat with her, and it was as if we already knew each other. In the course of these discussions, the Giants opened up a quick 7-0 lead in Game 7 against the Cardinals, making an improbable second trip to the World Series statistically more likely, partially on the strength of a Hunter Pence hit that seemed to have reverse sonar as it zigzagged away from the defender, shortstop Pete Kozma. (Steve passed up going; maybe next time — which does not sound so crazy anymore.) In that NLCS Game 7, watched mostly with my 15-year-old daughter Adrianna, I did not relax until it was over. As in *over* over. If the Cardinals scored one run in the ninth, I would have become unsettled, as if they might claw back the way they did in record fashion in the NLDS against the Washington Nationals. (My brother Bob is a Cardinals fan and we both were respectful in these days, avoiding trash talk.) Earlier in the evening, I had proposed that Adrianna, my wife Beth, and I pour Saratoga water on our heads if the Giants were to clinch (we don't drink booze), but the idea got vetoed mostly because our floors were refinished over the summer. (I offered to place plastic trash bags on the wooden floors, but the idea was nixed.)

Although I knew my flight to SF was to leave at 10:30 a.m. Tuesday and I needed to pack, I could not calm down. After the 9-0 Matt Cain pennant winner, I managed to settle down by washing a load of dishes around 12:40 a.m. It's my household chore. It more or less worked.

The next morning I left for the airport after dropping off Adrianna at school and saying goodbye to Beth. It was 46 degrees and drizzly, according to the lighted sign on the thoroughfare into Syracuse Hancock International Airport. At the airport's Gateway Cafe, Scott, the cook, noticed my hat and engaged in an animated conversation, talking about McCovey Cove and noting he was from Yosemite. All right! And before that, a United Airlines maintenance guy saw my gear and said, "Man, they crushed the Cardinals. I'm just hoping for seven games." Before that, my friend Derek, also known as Chicken, an electrician at Hancock, saw me and congratulated me, as did his fellow worker, Paul Delaney, who it turns out is a Giants fan who lived for a time in the Bay Area. Derek had just seen me about three weeks earlier, as I headed out to Tampa to promote my first book. Me, Mr. Big Shot.

As for the pilgrimage itself, in the busy O'Hare concourse terminals in Chicago, one passing traveler saw my Giants hat and neon orange 2010 World Champions sweatshirt and shouted with a smug smile "Go, Tigers!" which got an ostentatious laugh from me, the kind of laugh that says, "Yeah, sure, represent your team, but in your dreams, buster." (As in, Buster Posey.) Neither the flight from Syracuse to Chicago, nor the second leg, from Chicago to SFO, featured hints of fellow pilgrims. I noticed no SF hats or sweatshirts, except mine, which prompted minor conversation, from a Reds fan and a Giants fan (Laverne, from the Richmond District, who ended up sitting to my right on the flight). One of the flight attendants told me her husband was at the clinching, in the downpour, right along the third-base line and showed me a photo on her phone. "Why aren't you or he going to Game 1 then?" I asked her, and she rolled her eyes at the purported astronomical cost. I told her, as I would tell anyone, I was heading out to San Francisco without a ticket, without a prospect of a ticket, or even a prospect of a prospect of a ticket. I didn't care. I had done this in 2010 and it was worth it. I should add that within the past week I had gotten the brainstorm of trying to get press credentials for the World Series. Why not? It had worked in Pittsburgh earlier in the summer. I was a real author, wasn't I? Though not a beat writer. It was worth a shot. But a fellow named Liam of the Giants informed me in a phone call that October 4 was the deadline for that and one had to contact MLB, for which he gave me a phone number. I next spoke with a Taylor at MLB, to no avail. He suggested I email credentials@mlb.com, which would allegedly be read by someone named Lydia. I did that from the Syracuse airport, just before boarding. I am still waiting for the courtesy of a reply.

Laverne, 68, who looked more like 55, related she was coming back from a 12-day trip to China with her sister. She was retired from the accounting department of a law firm and enjoyed traveling the world. She shared some shortbread cookies with me. I did not manage to grab a lunch at O'Hare but bought cheese and crackers on the plane. Laverne gave me some travel tips for when I landed, suggesting I take the BART to Daly City and then a number 28 Muni bus. Not owning a car, she knew the transit system well. She told me the bus would travel with the cross streets in reverse alphabetical order. We landed at SFO around 3 p.m. local time. It is a cliché, but I am always taken by the Bay Area's light and air. I love seeing little wisps of floating fog in distant hills, like dust or powder. I felt World Series electricity in the air. Seeing my gear, Kevin, a customer service rep in the baggage area, noted he was a Tigers' fan going back to 1968 and the Mickey Lolich era. But his "Go, Giants" betrayed no severe inner conflict. Before going our separate ways, Laverne again asked if I knew what cross street from 11th Avenue Aunt Mary lived on. It so happened I was on the phone with Steve Melikean, and he said "Judah," so she said that should work well.

As suggested, I took the BART to Daly City and promptly got on a 28 bus, sitting up front near the driver. I asked him about directions, wondering whether I could have walked to my destination. Not readily or quickly, he noted. "You'd have to up the hill and all the way back down." Again, I had no understanding of scale or orientation. Without distracting the driver, I told him of my mission and my roots as a Giants fan harkening back to New York days. As we rode along 19th Avenue and I told him I needed to get off at Judah, I mentioned something about the reverse alphabetical order of the cross streets. It seemed to be a revelation and we had a good-natured laugh about that. For one brief moment in the late afternoon sun, I caught the top of the Golden Gate Bridge glinting ahead of us, the tops of two spires, the rest of the bridge hidden from view. A trompe l'oeuil of the natural world. I soaked it in, knowing I could not get my camera out fast enough and no photo from me would do the sight justice. I got off with my small black suitcase and Ogio shoulder bag at the corner of 19th and Judah. A tent was set up where off-market Giants and Niners shirts and hats were being sold at discount. For five dollars I bought a FU*K YEAH T-shirt for Adrianna. Did this make me a bad parent? I think not. (Later the next day, fellow fervent fans would also give me a free pass on that.) I declare this because the shirt did not technically have an obscenity. Where the C would be was an image of Tim Lincecum in full wind-up stride. A little history is in order: if I am not mistaken from my East Coast perch, when the Giants won the pennant in 2010, Amy Gutierrez, the on-field broadcast person, asked Timmy if he was going to celebrate, and he responded with a throaty "Fu*k yeah" and the whole of AT&T and its viewing audience heard it. T-shirts accordingly bloomed.

I wanted to walk, to stretch my jet-cabin-cramped legs and to feel the pavement, see the neighborhood, catch the smells and sounds. I texted and called home, when traffic sounds did not interfere. I called my mom, 96, in Connecticut as I ambled across the street from St. Anne of the Sunset Catholic Church, a spectacularly beautiful structure with ornate bas-relief sculptures of saints set against a pink-salmon background. I abbreviated the call as a train rolled by, the very one that I could have been riding had I chosen not to walk. I went up Judah Street from 19th Avenue and turned left onto 11th Avenue. I soon found the block on 11th Avenue I was searching for, just past Irving Street, and was struck by the neighborliness of the environs. It reminded me of Bayonne, New Jersey, which I had visited in the 1980s but which seemed more out of the 1950s. Irving features shops of broad diversity, Asian and Greek restaurants, nail salons, coffee shops, a creperie, and true to the Fifties, even a Rexall drugstore sign.

Arriving at my destination, I rang the buzzer. I heard barking dogs. A short, thin woman of almost olive complexion with a ready smile, Aunt Mary warmly greeted me and showed me around the house and the upstairs room that would be mine. I told her I needed to walk the neighborhood, and she came out with me, inviting me to join her and her house guests for supper at 7, which would be 10 p.m. back east. She proceed to the store, and I settled at Tart to Tart on Irving, where I retrieved emails, made calls, and sent and received texts. To my left, the sun was setting, bleaching out visibility up Irving Street. A bronze gauzy haze drenched the streetscape. I guess it really is the Sunset District, I said to myself in corny fashion.

Just before supper, I searched local stores for copies of the Chron. I wanted to see how the Game 7 pennant clincher from hours before was covered. (Is it possible? Could the pennant have been clinched mere hours before and I had hopped on a plane, possessed with manic euphoria but no game ticket?) A Sporting Green was not to be found. Then, at a corner liquor store-discount store near the corner of Irving and 11th Avenue, I asked the clerk if he had any.

"I've got five, but I had someone reserve them, my friend. I'm sorry."

"Oh, man, I understand. But let me at least look at them. Hey, I go back. I go back to the New York Giants. I came out here just for this."

The young fellow was impressed. We exchanged fist bumps. Darcy, a woman who seemed to be a regular or a friend at the counter, gave a friendly nod and smile.

"What's your name?"

"Mohammed."

"Paul."

He seemed genuinely moved. More fist bumps.

"We're so proud. What else is there that is better for an Iraqi-American," he said.

Our supper of bratwurst and vegetables was shared by Aunt Mary, 73; Francesca, 27, of Hamburg, Germany, a tall blonde law student; and Nadine, also 27, a brunette from Switzerland, who came to the U.S. on her own to increase her job prospects. I regaled the table with details of my journey, underscoring that I had come all this way without expecting any prospect at all of getting into the ballpark, and that was fine. The two young ladies floated some plans of finding a local bar to watch Game 1 on Wednesday. I noted it was likely I would not see them after this evening.

Mary related to me a curious baseball story. She described going to Seals Stadium when she was around 13 with her father. It was awful. The crowd, she said, was foul and vulgar. She never went back. She almost never again went to a game — not at Seals Stadium, not at Candlestick Park, and not at AT&T Park or any of its previous names, although she did see the Pope at Candlestick.

On Tuesday evening I received an email regarding a small editing project requiring quick turnaround for a firm back in Syracuse. That provided some distraction and assuaged my guilt over my expensive airfare. It was good for me, but the tasks at hand were only the veneer of civilization taming a wild animal ready to play and roar.

Chapter 6
WALKING THE EMBARCADERO

On Wednesday morning, October 24, the day of Game 1, I could not sleep, though it was 6:20 a.m. back home, where my biological clock still ticked. My too-early-awakeness was spurred by messages from the eastern front. Lenn "RaysFanGio" Fraraccio texted me "Giants in 6." Being up, I worked on my editing project. Then I went down Irving to the Crepevine restaurant, for one of the best breakfasts I've ever had. Roasted potatoes with rosemary, garlic, and olive oil, toasted sourdough bread, locally made jelly, probably the butter too, and a pot of robust breakfast tea whose leaves were put through a strainer. What could be better? That and reading the Sporting Green. This mirrored my pregame meditation-breakfast-game prep before Game 1 in 2010. As I did then, I called Beth and filed a brief but animated dispatch.

Reading in the morning San Francisco Chronicle about people's superstitions, I concluded I am a passionate fan but not very superstitious. On the way back to the apartment, I returned to Starbucks to buy a second copy of The Chronicle, to have reading material as I traveled during the day. I encountered an affable Tigers fan there.

Before boarding the N Judah train downtown to go to the Dugout Store and have lunch with Ted Speros, I talked baseball on my cell with RaysFanGio in Tampa. Gio is one of the stars of my first book. Then, on the moderately crowded Muni train headed downtown, I found a seat next to a young lady wearing sunglasses and Giants gear.

"Are you going to the game?" I asked her.

"No, I have to go to work down near there. You?"

"I'm going to just hang out by the ballpark and meet some friends. It'll be cool. Where do you work?"

"In the Ferry Building. Perry's."

"Oh, yeah, I'm familiar with the one on Union Street. I was there once, about a hundred years ago."

"I used to work at that one."

We talked about her reading. She had a paperback of Lolita by Vladimir Nabokov, and I related how I was an English major and we talked about City Lights bookstore. I had some copies of my book and was all too glad to lessen my load.

"What's your name?"

"Erika."

"With a 'c' or a 'k'?"

"A 'k'."

So I signed it, mumbling words about giving it to a friend or father or brother, if she wanted to, inscribing something like, "On the train, on the way to the World Series." Shameless promotion or flirting, or both. When the train arrived at the Embarcadero stop, I deliberately went in a different direction from her, so as not to appear creepy (even though I discovered I *should* have gone where she walked to get to the Dugout Store). The Dugout was frenzied and busy, even though it was about 11:30 in the morning. But it surely was a better option than the store at the ballpark, which I knew would be impossible to navigate and would eat up too much time just standing in lines. At the store I dropped over a hundred bucks without even trying. I had fun chatting it up with fellow fans in the line that snaked through the small outlet. In front of me was a woman who was a San Francisco firefighter. As I bordered on criticizing her cutting ahead, I was reminded she was on duty at lunchtime. Okay! Go for it!

I bought a sweatshirt for Beth, a panda hat and

winter ski hat for Adrianna, a World Series program, and as I neared the register, loudly repeating the phrase "impulse buy!" I added a pack of baseball cards and a keychain.

I texted Ted that I was finished at the store and would try to meet him on the street halfway from the Dugout to his bank on Sansome Street. "I'll have a suit on," he said. "And I'll have Giants gear," I replied. Right. As if those were good indicators. We both clicked off our phones and proceeded with no further directions. After taking some pictures of window displays cheerleading for the Giants at The Royal Exchange Restaurant and Sports Bar at the corner of Sacramento and Front Streets, I walked several yards and we practically bumped into each other. True, he had seen pictures of me on the blog, but come on! As Ted later related to me in an email, "I'll never forget the look on your face when you thought I was just some anonymous Giants fan admiring your hoodie."

We ate at the Holding Company Bar & Grill at the Embarcadero Center. Our warm and cordial conversation was partly about the Giants but also touched on personal elements of our lives.

"You have referred to your Chinese mother. What do you mean by that?"

"When I was a teenager, my single mom really could not afford to raise me. I went to live with a Chinese family. I became part of their family."

His story struck me as not only quintessentially American but particularly San Franciscan: a Greek-American raised by Chinese-Americans.

Ted is a true film buff. We talked about one of my favorites, "Mean Streets," his voiceover and acting roles, and his career since his teen years in banking. He had linguine with clams, I a juicy burger on sourdough. He paid. He insisted. I was his guest. After lunch, we hugged outside. We posed for pictures that a stranger took, with the TransAmerica Building in the background. I felt privileged to meet this man. Bonus: he handed me a business internal circulation envelope with Chronicle newspaper articles. It was not until I got back to Syracuse more than a week later that I saw the trove of great journalistic memorabilia, including headlines from Game 7 that I had been searching for the night before. This was followed days later by even more remarkable collector's items of special editions of the San Francisco Chronicle.

I had a few hours available before heading to AT&T to meet my friend Craig Vaughan. It was getting sunny and pleasant. A perfect day. I had no qualms whatsoever that I had no game ticket. In fact I was not going to waste psychic energy even allowing for the scenarios that would allow me to get a ticket. The Chron that morning had illustrated that it was impossible. Even standing-room tickets for people calling in "chips" from the mayor and all sorts of connected people could not be had. Someone in the Chron article report had offered to eat a cockroach to get a ticket! Not me. I would be content to meet a few folks from the blogosphere and soak in every molecule of fan excitement.

I crossed the street to the Ferry Building. As I did so, I asked a pedestrian, "What street is this?" "The Embarcadero," he said. Well, duh! I felt like the most touristy of tourists. I figured maybe it was what he said it was but was unclear if the whole "area" was so named or just the walkway or the road or all of that. I'm still not so sure of that nor do I care. But I felt like a moron. (Question: Would a New Yorker throw an F bomb in there if you had asked him the same sort of question while on Fifth Avenue?) In the Ferry Building I walked up the main entrance steps and surveyed an expanse of ornate hallways. A guard prevented me from going further, since I had no business to conduct, but we engaged in hearty pleasantries about the approaching game. Downstairs, amid the shops and kiosks of wineries and other crafted foodstuffs and organic products, I bought a cinnamon roll at Mariposa Baking Company, "artisan-crafted gluten-free," joking with the associate about artisan as a word. "I get it. I call myself an artisanal wordsmith on LinkedIn." "Enjoy," she amiably urged me.

The next mile or two offered me supreme and simple joy. I walked in back of the Ferry Building out onto the pier. I had never done this before. I enjoyed the solitude and the view of the Bay Bridge, the water sparkling and the cars and trucks overhead quietly traversing back and forth over the water. Seagulls abounded. I spotted a man smoking a cigar.

"A cigar. Sir, can you tell me where you bought that? I could go for a good cigar right about now."

He pulled out a leather holder and offered me a cigar, a JR.

"No, no, you don't have to do that. Really."
"Not at all. Here."

I gladly accepted a cigar and he gave me some matches. When I had some trouble in the breeze, I walked over to the back of a store and a woman let me use her lighter. I walked back over to the gentleman along the water who had given me a cigar. We introduced each other, exchanging business cards. I told him how my older daughter, Evelyn, a ballet dancer, had been to France, even almost worked there. Stéphane Prunet is an investment manager for Manifold Partners LLC at the Ferry Building. I told him why I was there, sans billet.

"You're a real fan, then."

"I guess you could say that. It will be fun. I've done this before. You can understand. It'd be like seeing Marseille, your football team."

We parted ways. I continued strolling down the Embarcadero toward the ballpark, calmly enjoying a fine cigar. I carried a brown bag from the Dugout Store with a few copies of my book, the souvenirs I had bought, the cinnamon roll, and the Chronicles that Ted had given me.

I sat down on a bench, almost under the San Francisco-Oakland Bay Bridge. The cigar not only relaxed me, it had a pleasant aroma and flavor. More, it added to a pregame sense of triumph, the way a Red Auerbach cigar would for the Celtics. When Red fired up his cigar, a Celtics victory was assured. I guess I felt like victory was in the air. This pause on a city bench on the Embarcadero served as a meditation. Take it all in. Know that this is good and savor it. Near my bench, a young woman was arranging outdoor tables for a restaurant. I apologized for the smoke. She waved it off, noting I was outdoors. I told her of my World Series trek. I'd tell anyone, wouldn't I?

Along the walk, I encountered a father and son. I demanded that I take their picture because they looked so perfect together, a modern-day Norman Rockwell scene. I met two Asian fellows. I insisted I have a picture taken with them. And I met one guy from Reno, asking him if he was "Dirtrocksnreno" from the blog. He was not. Good cheer was in the air. Speaking of air, I took the last few drags of my now-tiny cigar and tossed it into the murky water, with seagulls fighting for it. I felt a tad shabby for that.

My walk resumed, I picked up the pace owing to my growing excitement. I walked into Red's Java House, operating since 1918, as the sign said. I had never heard of it, but it was buzzing with fans. I bought a cup of java. Why not? I have not had booze since 1979 and wouldn't one want a cup of real java here? I used the restroom and enjoyed the retro black and white photos, the kind that features the Rat Pack. Cadillacs, cigarettes, and martinis. I crept back toward the back patio and took a few pictures of the ballpark through a chain-link fence. I started a chat with two guys at an outdoor table because one had a Mays jersey on. With them, I traced my journey to this table, from Mays until now. John and John, two guys sharing a beer before the game. The other guy looked like he could be Matt Cain's father. He knew it, had been told it before. I think he had Cain's autograph on his number 18 jersey. The three of us marveled at how the Giants got here. What could be better than this, right now? We all agreed.

A coffee from Red's Java House in hand, I marched onward to AT&T Park. I got a text from Craig. He was running a little late from Palo Alto Hills. I texted back that I was running a bit late myself, owing to conversations along the way, which would surprise no one. Craig was an important motivation for me to make the trip to San Francisco, not just because he ran a Giants blog. I had met him near McCovey Cove before Game 1 of the 2010 World Series. He said if I could fly across the country for this, the least he could do is come out and greet me. Knowing someone at my shrine destination anchored me and gave me a sense of comfort. I knew I would not wander aimlessly trying to engage in fan talk with strangers.

I was thrilled to be approaching the stadium in a completely new way. I enjoyed the banners along the roadway celebrating the Giants' playoff run. Images of Sandoval, Posey, Romo. The boats in the marina to my left gleamed on the water. I followed the path of the pedestrian promenade, occasionally taking pictures, forwarding them from my phone, or asking strangers to take my photo. It was nearing 3 p.m., still more than two hours before Game 1. Plenty of time to absorb the atmosphere. Plenty of time to get used to a faster pulse.

Chapter 7

TO THE CATHEDRAL STEPS

Cruising into the environs of AT&T Park on October 24, 2012, I discerned an atmosphere of buoyancy and brightness, a climate of triumph no matter what would transpire in the ballgame. I felt included, part of a proud community. I detected little of the anger of some other fan bases, the kind arrogant anger that says, "I told you so" or the resentful anger that says "we deserve more." I say that, but that is a bit of wishful thinking. I would be lying if I said otherwise. Some pockets of fans exhibited both of those traits, especially toward the national media.

Plans called for me to meet Craig by the Willie Mays statue, so I ambled from the outer reaches of the marina, more or less in back of left field, in back of center, and then along McCovey Cove. Spying through the Knothole, where I spent a few innings in 2010, I saw some players warming up on the field. Just as at my first game more than 50 years earlier in Yankee Stadium, the players seemed awash in luminous glow, on a grass greener than anywhere else. I saw the Knothole line and repeated to myself the vow that I would not do that again. I was not up for standing around. One heavyset, older guy camped at the front of the Knothole line told me it was a good vantage point to watch people all day, since noon. Nope, I told myself, not for me. Not this time.

I arrived at the Mays point of convocation around 3:30. No Craig. Since he is 6 foot 6 he is easy to spot. It was surprisingly uncrowded by the statue. ESPN set up a booth nearby for live broadcasts with Karl Ravech, Curt Schilling, John Kruk, and others. The fans were merciless toward Schilling. I personally have always found it hard to forgive and forget how he campaigned for George W. Bush right after the 2004 World Series victory with the Red Sox. We taunted him about putting ketchup on his "bloody" sock. Stuff like that. At one point, the ESPN people said they were going live, exhorting us to go wild. It was instructive in the use, and misuse, of modern mass communications. For one thing, there were not many of us there in front of the swooping-down camera. Second, we were not that rowdy. Nevertheless, when the red light went on, there we were, myself included, gawking and grimacing and whooping and hollering. I did not know what to do. I gave a lame point of my index finger and a thumbs up. I felt like an idiot. It just wasn't me, not at this age at least. I called home to alert them to this, and they were not at home and did not see it, fortunately. I called my friend Tom Coman, and he later revealed he saw it when ESPN did this again moments later and I was front and center. Destroy the tapes, Tom.

Within a few moments, Craig was on the scene. We exchanged hugs and handshakes.

"I can't believe when you said weeks ago at the Flap how happy you'd be to see me again for the World Series that this really happened. It really came true" I enthused. He and I overheard some of the ESPN chatter, and all the invective it brought. We agreed they were pretty much full of crap, at least from what we could hear. We both appeared briefly on the ESPN live feed, if only in the background. We then took a leisurely walk around the park perimeter, stopping near the Juan Marichal statue for me to sign a copy of *Baseball's Starry Night*. He generously overpaid $20 for it, insisting on it. We walked along the promenade near the Knothole, and I told Craig I did not know what I was going to do during the game, didn't know where I'd watch it, but it would not be the Knothole viewing fence. We walked out near a breakwater into the bay that I had never noticed before. A couple took our picture. The breakwater, I could see, was what made McCovey Cove so calm. When Craig and I were out there, in the lambent late afternoon light, we got to know each other a bit. He gave me some detail about the sort of work he does, his efforts with children with behavioral problems. It all sounded terribly challenging. Craig strikes me as a person of authority, not just by virtue of his size. He has a solidity in belief and practice. I know he coaches girls' soccer, and I can see he has leadership and mentoring qualities that are surely effective.

Part of Craig's mission was to find a brick that Bozo's family had bought around the stadium pedestrian areas. We tried to track it down as if on a treasure hunt, with no luck. Craig also specifically wanted to find the plaque in the ground commemorating Matt Cain's perfect game in June 2012. We found it out in back by the Cove and took some pictures.

When we circled back to the Mays statue, Craig and I connected with our mutual friend Micah Oliveira and his dad, Joe. It was Micah's birthday. His wife insisted that she get him tickets to go to the game, so there he was with his dad. We all posed for pictures, and I was happy for them, not too jealous that they were getting in to the game. Once Micah and Joe left because they were itching to get into the stadium, Craig and I walked against the flow of the crowd on the King Street sidewalk adjacent to the ballpark. The rapper Roach Gigz and his crew came rolling by on a skateboard a few feet from us as they filmed a video. (I cannot see us in the music video making the rounds, though I scoured the footage as if it were the Zapruder film of the JFK assassination.) Craig and I sat down near the Orlando Cepeda statue, just to enjoy the crowd before he headed back to the Palo Alto area. Our conversation was not entirely about baseball, because there were pulchritudinous sights to divert our attention. Out of nowhere, we heard a "Craig, is that you?" It turned out to be Jordana, a woman Craig had not seen in maybe 10 years. I enjoyed their conversation and meeting her, even joking that she might want to be generous and let me have one of her tickets. Craig talked of wanting to get back home; responsibilities were calling. He would soon be taking a bullet train back home in time to catch most of the game. I offered to walk with him toward the train. We walked on King Street toward Third Street.

Then my eye caught some big money changing hands on the sidewalk of King between a bald-headed white guy and a black guy with a hat.

"Are you selling tickets?"

"How much you want to pay?" the black fellow, the man with tickets in his hand, replied.

I had not imagined this scenario, or anything like it.

"Uh, three hundred dollars," I said, knowing full well that any good poker player does not bid with an "um" or an "uh." In the midst of this flash of excitement, fear, and nervousness, I bobbed my head left to Craig and right to my negotiators. Craig was en route to his train. It was less than twenty minutes to game time.

"Craig, what do you think? Do you think it's legit?"

The entrepreneur let me hold the ticket and inspect it. I had heard and read about counterfeit tickets. Was this all a scam?

"Yeah, go for it, dude. 150. You're just one ticket, and it's close to game time."

"Two hundred."

"All right, man."

What happened next was so lightning-fast, I cannot vouch for its accuracy. Plus, everything was imbued with an electric aura of fear and trembling and anticipation (like sex for the first time, hahaha).

I said to the guy with the shaved head, who apparently was upgrading from tickets he had to be with his son and have better seats (to this day I can't figure it out), "You have to walk into the stadium with me, okay? You have to be there, in case it's bogus."

"Sure, sure," the man who told me his name was Barry said. (As if that would mean anything if his ticket was good and mine was not. I can just picture the scene at the turnstile, "See ya!" he says and walks on with a big grin.)

"Okay, okay, wait a second. I need to go to the ATM over here."

I walk to the corner of Third and King. There's a lot of movement, hustle and bustle, shirts being sold, fans milling about. The street guy stands near me, rushing me. I can hardly read the screen in the glare of the sun. I try to shade it with my hand. Street Guy is coaxing, coaching, pushing me, telling me which buttons to press. My hands are shaking. I am now fairly certain that I have made a dangerous and stupid decision. I don't know what happened to Craig. He's gone. I punch in the wrong info on the ATM machine, and I am afraid the machine will eat my card. I try again. I am asked to accept a surcharge of $3.50. I accept. At 4:54:55 p.m., the machine dispenses $200 in cash. I make the deal with Street Guy. I have the ticket, or piece of paper purporting to be a ticket. Street Guy and Guy Who Says He Is Barry then engage in a private, heated conversation. This makes me more nervous and scared. Street Guy asks me to "help him out a little," because after all he helped me out, as he put it. I want to tip him but I am paranoid. I fish out a five-dollar bill, feeling cheap and disrespectful while simultaneously feeling I may have thrown all this money away. Guy Who Says He Is Barry and I start across the street toward the Willie Mays gate. A roar and rumble that sinks into my chest almost buckles my knees. It's the pregame flyover of fighter jets. I walk toward the Willie Mays Gate entrance, still terrified I will not get in but also thrilled that I might.

Chapter 8

PANDALIRIOUS!

As I am walking toward the entrance to the Willie Mays Gate at AT&T Park minutes before Game 1 of the 2012 World Series, Guy Who Says He Is Barry, the middle man involved in my "ticket" purchase, tells me something about not to worry, he traded tickets, they almost got arrested earlier, and what-not. None of this settles my nerves. We get in line to enter the stadium. I don't know if I'm going to get arrested, a far-fetched result, or present my ticket at the turnstile and be told it is fraudulent and invalid. The line shuffles along steadily. Everyone looks buoyant. I look scared. Guy Who Says He Is Barry is to my right. The ticket is for the bleachers. First, my bag with all the stuff from the Dugout store gets searched. Passed. Then a few feet farther, the turnstile with people scanning tickets. The woman takes my ticket and looks at it. My heart beats then stops. My hands shake but not visibly, I hope. She scans the ticket. She pauses. She says nothing, and if she did say anything it would have been drowned out by the roar of hydroelectric tension coursing through my head. The turnstile lets me through. I'm in.

Guy Who Says He Is Barry gives a look like, what was your problem? Easy! "Where are you sitting?" he asks. I show him my ticket. "I'll come over and see you during the game if I can."

From a large cardboard carton I grab my Giants orange hankie to wave. How cool is that? This is for real. I can be one of those crazy orange-hankie-waving fans! I also get a cardboard banner from ComcastSportsnet that says AUTHENTIC FAN with the Giants logo. That I am, that I am. I also receive a Stand Up 4 Cancer placard to hold up during the game and a rubber bracelet supporting the same. The National Anthem has already been sung by someone. Barry Zito has thrown the first pitch. I walk along the concourse of the club level with my heart racing, trading glances from television screens at food concessions to glimpses of the field. With unsteady hands I text my triumph back home. I hear bits and pieces of play-by-play echoing. By the roars or the groans of the crowd, I get an inkling of favorable or dreadful in-game results. From what I can discern, at least no disaster is impending and maybe Zito can continue his postseason Zen mastery, as he did when he forced the Cardinals to travel back to San Francisco in the NLCS.

I make my way from the home plate area to the first base and right field sections. Near the arcade outfield area I look out toward McCovey Cove and the throngs milling around the perimeter of the ballpark and the moody clouds in the dusk with a construction crane in the beyond. I am trying to fathom how I have become one of the Elect, one of the Chosen People of Giants Fans.

Just before getting to my bleachers area, Section B142, I stop at the bathroom and then I buy a Peet's Coffee, at $4.25, for two reasons: I want a coffee and I want to have a drink in my hand as a practical tool to safeguard sobriety. I gab with the woman behind the Centerplate concession counter, sharing my story of disbelief that I am here, here, here, now, now, now. My hands by this time may have been visibly unsteady. All the while the game is going on, and I gather that Zito survives the top of the first working out of mild trouble. We can win this.

Arriving at Section B142, Row 28, sometime in the bottom of the first, my shyness and ticket-purchase nervousness made me feel as if I might be intruding on someone's party. The seat was wet, presumably from wet beer. I put down a plastic bag I brought with me in the morning, from Aunt Mary's, onto the metal bench. That protective seat covering lasted about five minutes as it ended up among the detritus. I introduced myself to some folks around me, trumpeting my long-distance-fan status. The close-knit "community" seemed to shift a bit, such that I thought it might be in so much flux as to be distracting. I felt it might consist of random people drifting raucously in and out, whereby I'd have to fight to maintain my own little patch of standing ground.

Pablo Sandoval's home run in the first erased any concerns about anything and put us all in a fine mood, punctuated by panoramic high-fives. The blast went to our left. (I was in left center, almost as far back as any seat in the outfield, not too far from the gigantic glove and the huge Coke bottle in left/left center.) Pablo's blast passed from our line of vision, so we could not tell it was a homer until cheers went up. Some people might've had the benefit of scoreboard video, at least after the fact. For me, it was very hard to see what was on the centerfield video screen, because of being so close and because of the angle of viewing. Sandoval's home run eerily echoed the first game of the World Series in 2010, when the Giants built a lead against Cliff Lee, one of the best pitchers in baseball. This time, Kung Fu Panda hit a home run off Justin Verlander, who was being called the best pitcher on the planet. It is not an exaggeration to compare the home run to Willie Mays's famous catch off Vic Wertz in Game 1 of the 1954 Series (as I have related, I was alive but have zero memory of this). Both events changed the climate. Both events rejiggered the predictive calculations that assigned the status of "favored" on two teams, the Cleveland Indians and Detroit Tigers, respectively. By the time of the second homer, and then the improbable third rocket, we were Pandalirious. With Pablo's third home run, we celebrated not merely through raucous yelling and hand slaps but a few earnest hugs, the kind you see in pictures of people at Times Square after World War II.

When Pablo came up for his potential fourth home run, everyone instinctively started chanting "FOUR FOUR FOUR FOUR FOUR" with four fingers raised. I can't say it was just the bleachers. Probably the whole ballpark. Could television viewers hear it? FOUR FOUR FOUR FOUR FOUR! But amidst this chanting litany it seemed to me that there were silent pauses with people just saluting with the four fingers raised and pumped. These silent intervals were chilling because of the contrast. The four fingers pulsating in unison seemed to signify the salute of a new nation. Pandalirious Nation.

As with 2010, we did not have to utter a syllable: it could happen again, we could win it all again for the second time in three years. How crazy is that? Ever since the string of elimination games in the NLDS and the NLCS, the Giants had had their backs to the wall. How sweet it was to be in the lead. And even though Sandoval singled instead of homered in his fourth at-bat, the lead we opened up against Verlander was a take-that-national-media delicious delight. Yummy. (Consider that Mr. Verlander thus far in the postseason had gone 3-0 with a 0.74 ERA and 25 strikeouts in nearly 25 innings.) Our don't-stop-believing was neither irrational faith nor fan hysteria.

Regarding Verlander, our bleacher people responded with a litany of throaty "Overrated" chants. Other taunts from our perch included shouts to the Tigers' center fielder, Austin Jackson. Like a crew coxswain, someone in back of me (you could not go much farther back in the house) would prompt, "What's the matter with Jackson?" and our antiphonal response in this cathedral was, "He's a bum!" After five or six times of this, the coda would be "Tigers suck!" but I feel that such chants were the extent of not-for-families or vulgar demonstrations; pretty mild for bleacher antics. I have heard worse in a school parking lot.

It was definitely our own world out there. And I was thrilled to inhabit it.

Chapter 9

YOLO KINGS AND QUEENS

As I started overcoming shyness and began to feel like a part of the hometown crew, I began to blurt out portions of my story, my journey, burnishing my credentials as a legacy fan, not that anyone cared or needed such a visa to grant acceptance. "YOLO," I yelled out goofily. "Yeah, you only live once." Now my surrounding cadre began to see the goofball antics they were in for. No matter. All was merry.

Being at the game, you not only get the sights and smells and asides and chatter of the people, you also get the music between innings while television viewers or radio listeners or Internet followers are on commercial break. One half inning featured a fist pump number from the cable show "Jersey Shore," or so I was told. So I obediently pumped my fist in the air with my orange Giants hankie. Later in the game, after we all went nuts with "Gangnam Style," the summer's worldwide mega-hit music video of Korean pop on YouTube, I used that as an excuse to indulge my hypercaffeinated state by randomly blurting out "Gangnam Style" at any time for no reason or to shout out such irrational exuberance as "hashtag torture" (in the ninth inning, after George Kontos gave up a two-run home run to Jhonny Peralta, making me nervous with a potentially tight score of 8-3) and then "hashtag victory" as we approached that reality, as if I were a possessed Twitter machine on speed. My bleacher people did not mind at all, not that I could tell. "Together we are Giant" as the slogan for the 2012 season declared.

We stood most of the time. For all of nine innings, I might have sat, a total of five minutes. Between half innings early on, I thought I would try to go to the rest room. The line was too long. I returned to my place and taught my body that you really can control your bladder. It was not an issue at all — this from someone who typically gets up two or three times a night. Being excited and voluble, of course I announced that I had to go to the bathroom but chose to forgo that option. "Thanks, for that" the lady in front with her man said with good humor. "No, no, it won't be anything like that. You don't have to worry about that," I replied, calming any jokey fears about urinary dysfunction. This is what it was like: repartee and jokes and shouts and chants and shrieks and even silences.

Late in the game, my body reminded me I was hungry, that I had not eaten since a full-bodied lunch at the Holding Company with Ted. I still had a cinnamon bun from Mariposa, a little shop in the Ferry Building.

I shouted that out to my crew, and the woman in front of me, whose name I never got, shouted back, "Oh, you're having a vegan doughnut? We're all about that in San Francisco, but we love it." When I bought the bun, those many hours earlier, I had joked with the owner or associate about the word "artisanal," telling her that on my LinkedIn profile I often refer to myself as an "artisanal wordsmith." Indeed I woofed down the last of my "vegan cinnamon doughnut" with the last draughts of the coffee I had bought in the first inning.

We deliriously chanted "Barry, Barry, Barry" for Zito as he exited in the top of the sixth inning. Other chants abounded, such as "Mar-co Scoooooo-tar-o." I learned the hand-on-the-head-held-vertically sign for the White Shark, Gregor Blanco, who made at least two sensational catches right below us. We chanted "Timmy, Timmy, Timmy" even as he warmed up.

I became a frantic, antic ringleader in my bleacher section. When Hunter Pence came to bat or when he made a play in right field, I vigorously shouted "Preacherman!" and "Reverend!" and "Elmer Gantry!" This was because Pence had become famous in the postseason for his rousing pregame pep talks to his teammates. He exhorted his fellow Giants like an Old Testament prophet, with eyes bulging out and teammates hugging in a circle in the dugout. "Play for the guy next to you. Play another day. I love this team." This would be followed by confetti hurled in the form of sunflower seeds, popcorn, and whatnot in a blizzard of wonderful, sophomoric verve. So, Hunter Pence acquired from the Philadelphia Phillies on July 31 at the trade deadline for 2010 stalwart Nate Schierholtz and minor-league catcher Tommy Joseph, had become the high priest of this Giants team.

Unlike the 2010 team, memorialized as a Band of Misfits in a book by Andrew Baggarly, the San Francisco Giants of the 2012 World Series run were — what? — Band of Brothers? And the Rt. Rev. Mr. Pence, for whom a bobblehead night in Philadelphia had to be scrapped, became a fierce leader to compare with the quiet, steady leadership of catcher Buster Posey. Mr. Pence, whose bat-breaking, bat-naming antics and praying-mantis, wiry approach at bat and in the field somehow got it done.

In our micro-bleacher community, we got to know each other. To my immediate right were newlyweds Danielle and Mike Johnston. I learned she is a special education language arts middle-school teacher and, having been an English teacher myself long ago, I exchanged some tidbits, such as declaring I'd use Twitter to teach her kids English. She related how she and Mike were in Australia last time around and considered going back to Australia for good luck. Good thing they did not, or else the story would not be the same.

Right in back of me were Kate van Bronkhorst and Sarah Zoucha, whose names I collected via Twitter, once

I told them my @kocakwords handle. It was they who recounted how they had been good-luck charms for the Giants, winning the last seven times they were at a game. These became "my girls." Their good-luck winning streak included the pennant clincher at AT&T Park, with the game ending in a deluge that Danielle and Mike and Kate and Sarah and anyone else who was there described as gloriously wet and who-the-hell-cares.

In back of me, next to Katie and Sarah were also Ryan (female name) and Daniel, I believe. At some point, Kate and Sarah anointed me as a companion good-luck charm. I cemented this status when before or during a Barry Zito at bat, I proclaimed, "He's going to hit a single, to left!" And he did. Of course, in my lack of humility I could not refrain from yelling, "I called it, I called it, I called it!"

As the game proceeded, if a high-five moment came along, I did corny stuff like raise my hands up, palms facing outward in back of me so that "my girls" could slap my hands and we did not even have to look at each other, as if this was our well established protocol.

There were solemn moments. We sang "God Bless America" in subdued fashion along with the civic servants who led us. There were lyrical moments, with the Orange October citizens swaying romantically to "When the Lights Go Down in the City" by Journey, with Mike and Danielle next to me all seriously hugging and kissing, which made me a tiny bit jealous, for 1.3 seconds.

In the end, the Giants won, 8-3. All was right with the world. Sure, it was just one game, but it was a big win. I wandered off toward the big Coke bottle and a broadcast booth set up out there. I was emotional and revved up. Then, as if in the back of another room as a party is emptying out, I heard fragments of singing. "The loveliness of Paris seems somehow sadly gay. The glory that was Rome is of another day." It was as if I'd forgotten about this part of the liturgical ritual, the recording of Tony Bennett singing "I Left My Heart in San Francisco." Yes, that was what I was hearing, the victory song. It came over the loudspeakers as the stadium was bathed in bright glow, with some wind and mist whipping up. I motioned toward Sarah and moved my hand in a twisting motion near my eyes to indicate "tears." I don't know if she got what I meant. I walked back toward my crew, at our seats, even though most of the folks had dispersed toward exits, souvenir stands, or restrooms. I found an isolated spot, if you can use that word to describe a venue that moments earlier held nearly 43,000 people. I sat on the metal bleacher. Tony Bennett sang. I put my head down, covered my face in my hands, and wept. I mean, *sobbed*.

.

Epilogue
A DROP OF DEW

I am glad I made a pilgrimage that ended with great tears of jubilation, relief, vindication, and pride. (That's a lot of labels. Maybe I was just tired and hormonal. Come on! Testosterone can make you weep.) What if the Giants had lost Game 1? What if I never got into the ballpark? (Worse yet, what if I was out two hundred bucks and in cuffs for breaking a local ordinance?) I will never know. I suspect being there was enough and more. When people visit a holy shrine, they can still have a good time minus the plenary indulgence, right? But that is easy to say now. And fraudulent. I was thrilled to be on the winning side, brimming with joy at overcoming the odds. The Giants beat the favored Detroit Tigers in cinematic and historic fashion. Who could ask for more?

Best of all was being there. As I proved to myself in 2010, the atmosphere of the environs was sufficient to electrify me. A land of milk and honey and a bit of mist and fog.

On my office wall is a plaque celebrating the 2010 World Series championship. I cannot help but see it frequently, day or night. I honestly figured, that's it. That's our one World Series in my lifetime. I'll take it. Finally. We made it to the top of the mountain. But the god of surprises tricked me. We won it all again in 2012, and I was there again.

There are moments in life when you are happy, you know you are happy, and you know you will remember being happy. Some of those moments are long, as in 3 hours 26 minutes — and counting.

Gratitude to the Unknown Instructors

What they undertook to do
They brought to pass;
All things hang like a drop of dew
Upon a blade of grass.

William Butler Yeats